Stacy Kellams

Five Seconds of Fear	5
Overcoming a Life of Limitation	11
Kinetic Thinking Closes the Gap	14
How to Create Authority	20
"The Kellams Theory of Kinetic Thinking"	20
How These "INs" Can Cause	25
Coming to the Table	30
WHAT ARE IMPORTANT ACTION ITEMS PRIOR TO THE NEGOTIATION?	41
WHAT IS MOTIVATING THE NEGOTIATION?	43
THE RISKS INVOLVED IN ANY NEGOTIATION	48
THE FACE-TO-FACE NEGOTIATION	51
THE POWER OF READING	56
BODY LANGUAGE AND HOW TO READ IT	58
WHAT IS NEURO-LINGUISTING PROGRAMMING?	64
THE POWER OF THE EMOTIONAL CLIMATE	66
THE POWER OF POWER	68
THE POWER OF CHARISMA	71
THE TACTICS	71
THE SILENT STRATEGY	74
THE RED HERRING OR DECOY	74
THE OLDEST TRICK IN THE BOOK-	77
BECAUSE THAT'S THE RULE	81
KNOWLEDGE	83
OPTIONS	86
COMPETITION	88

HOW DO YOU CUT DOWN ON YOUR OWN COMPETITION AND REDUCE NEGOTIATIONS? 90

THE RUN AROUND 92

THE HOSTILE NEGOTIATOR 93

THE WALK OUT 94

CASH IN HAND 96

JUST TRY IT FOR THE WEEKEND 98

WHY THE HELL NOT? 100

WHAT PISSES THE OTHER PARTY OFF 102

The Never Ending Negotiation 105

THE HIGHER AUTHORITY 107

GET OUT THERE AND START 109

WARNING!

REPRODUCTION OF THESE COPYRIGHTED PRINTED MATERIALS ARE PROHIBITED BY LAW.

Copyright © 2016 Negotiate For Life.

All material is protected under federal and state copyright laws. This document is unpublished and the foregoing notice is affixed to protect Probate Possibilities in the event of inadvertent publication. All rights reserved. No part of this document may be reproduced in any form, including but not limited to photocopying or transmitting electronically to any computer, without the prior written consent of Probate Possibilities. The information contained in this document is confidential and proprietary to Probate Possibilities, and may not be used or disclosed except as expressly authorized in writing by Probate Possibilities. That means; YOU MAY NOT SELL, TRADE, COPY, ASSIGN, LEASE or LICENSE the rights to these materials under any circumstance.

Reproduction or translation of any part of this work without the permission of the copyright owner is unlawful and will be prosecuted to the full extent of the law.

TRADEMARKS

Company names and product names mentioned in this document are trademarks or registered trademarks of their respective owners and are hereby acknowledged.

LEGAL DISCLAIMER

I am not an attorney and you should seek the advice of a legal professional if you have specific legal questions regarding your state's practices. This training manual is based on Texas law and the Texas system. Other states may be different, but the overall process is the same. Each individual state and furthermore each individual county handles probate a little differently.

PUBLICATION DISCLAIMER

Negotiate For Life assumes no responsibility for errors, inaccuracies, or omissions that may appear in this publication. Negotiate For Life reserves the right to change this publication at any time without notice. This publication is not to be construed as conferring by implication, estoppels, or otherwise any license or right under copyright or patent whether or not the use of any information in this publication employs material claimed in any copyrighted work or an invention claimed in any existing or later issued patent.

Pumpjack Publishing COPYRIGHT © 2016

CHAPTER 1

Five Seconds of Fear

I had a friend in college who used to tell me that if you can get through the first five seconds of any situation, you would be able to quickly grab hold of it and complete the task. In a negotiation of any kind, it's not uncommon for your autonomic nervous system to let you know it is in charge. Your pulse will race a bit, your hands might get sweaty. You will feel nervous in general. This is normal, frankly, what you fear is the unknown.

As you know, there are different types of negotiations, how do I talk this woman at Starbucks out of her phone number (which still might cause your cheeks to flush) or, how to I get the best price on this house because I already know I have a fantastic contractor who will turn will make it worth fair market. Either way, your body will respond. Few people are calm, cool and collected when faced with the unknown results of a situation and the unknown personality of the other party.

I've tested this theory hundreds of time and I use it along with a similar strategy and that is to walk right up to my fear and watch it fall away. Fears are generally caused by the unknown and we all have fears which are justified and those that are somewhat unrealistic.

For example, some people have a fear of speaking in public. If they have tried and failed, the fear is justified. If they have never spoken in public it's more fear of the unknown keeping them paralyzed.

I'm not speaking about the fear we might feel when we wake to find someone has invaded our home. That is legitimate and rational fear. What I recognized as fear of the "unknown" is almost maddening and it can grow quickly into something entirely unmanageable. So, as with most other strategies I use, taking small bites of an elephant is far easier than trying to eat it whole.

The easiest way to deal with fear of the unknown is to get to know every facet of the experience. Scuba diving? Read up on it, talk to people who have gone, research the marine life you will encounter on your first open dive, take the certification course and then immerse yourself slowly.

Enter "The Kellams Theory of Kinetic Thinking." I've launched this concept recently to help people understand how to get "from here to there," "from A to B," "to start their own business," "to define and reach goals," "to confront fear with knowledge and tackle it."

"The Kellams Theory of Kinetic Thinking," depends on active thought. So, let's put our ideas into motion and pin-point how we get rid of fear in order to move in a more positive direction in all aspects of our lives.

1) Identify all the areas in which you feel you are being held back. It could be financially due to the lack of a promotion long over due. It could be a sore back preventing you from managing your weight. It could be an estranged relationship. It could be the desire to quit your job and become a real estate investor.
2) Determine why you feel you are being held back. In the above scenarios it could be fear of failure, fear of injury, fear of rejection and fear of walking away from a "known" and heading into a new career field. These are all reasonable concerns.
3) Identify the reasons you might be feeling those fears. In the above scenarios it might be that you've already interviewed twice and been passed over, you've gone to therapy and thus far nothing has lessened the pain in your back, and you've reached out via email to the estranged

person and not been acknowledged. Real estate investing is what you always wanted to do, yet the people you know who are real estate investors are wildly successful and you don't know how to get THERE. So, there is some legitimate fear based on past experience.

NOW, for Kinetic thinking. We need, in each instance to establish the reasons why the previous results might have been negative and what, moving forward we might be able to change in our approach that could produce a better result.

Let's just take the interview vignette. If you'd gotten no feedback from your superiors as to why you were not given the position, make an appointment and ask why. If you are still given no feedback that might help you to take a different route insert a positive reason such as there might have been a better candidate at the time. Moving forward, begin preparing for a third interview, make certain you are solid on all fronts, whether that requires you to research all aspects of the job you are interviewing for, getting to know the people who currently that position, read some books on interview techniques and see where you honestly think you might have failed. Another idea would be to practice interviewing with friends you might have who interview for their companies. I once googled the top fifty interview questions and worked through them all to the point I could answer them without thinking. How many have come up? Not a ton. But I still felt capable going into any presentation, negotiation, or when I interviewed or was interviewed.

This is Kinetic thinking and it WORKS. Positive thinking and happy thoughts will only take you so far. You must invest in your dreams and this is not and never will be passive- it is active. You can not feel your way to your goals, but your can work on your goals to feel better and more positive.

The reason I've brought up every day situations, is to demonstrate how we negotiate everyday. You want a raise. Your boss doesn't want to give you one. You are nervous about asking for one. This involves a negotiation and you must put into play the Kellams Theory of Kinetic Thinking and get to work. Examine your career with the company from start to present. Know what contributions you have made, if you are in a sales position, what sales have you made and how much have they benefited the company?

If you are in advertising, how significant a contribution have the campaigns you worked on been to the reputation of the firm? If you want to be partner at your law firm, you had better come to the negotiation table with both guns loaded. You have to have a proven track record of bringing in new business and billing. Of course your work ethic and time spend at the office will be evidenced by your billing. The point to all of this is whether you want an extra shot of espresso in your coffee at no charge because your coffee was not as hot as it should have been last time- ASK. There is no harm in asking.

You have done the first step to learn about negotiating- this course will help give you the confidence moving forward as you are faced with one negotiation after another.

Be ACTIVE. BE Kinetic. MOVE.

CHAPTER 2

Overcoming a Life of Limitation

As adults we are a product of our upbringing, whether we want to admit it or not. Our very first coaches were our parents and our extended family. Teachers, counselors and athletic coaches became our assistant coaching team. From the very beginning we had people teaching, nurturing, educating and pushing us to succeed.

However, each of those coaches had their own areas of expertise and they taught from a place of strength. We, as little sponges learned to internalize and act on those life lessons.

Have you ever had a moment when you suddenly remember the impact a certain teacher had on you or something a close family friend imparted to you? I have, often in fact, mostly it's a little saying I hear in my grandfather's voice.

So, does it make any sense that once we become "adults" we would no longer need guidance and coaching? It's why you bought this course and I applaud you for recognizing no matter how much you THINK you already know about business and negotiating, there is still more to learn and I'm certain there will be things covered in this course you might not have thought of.

As adults we need coaching and mentoring more than ever as we embark on creating and maintaining relationships, learning how to build a business network, how to thrive in our new career, figuring out how to balance work and home obligations, and how to cope with our metabolism beginning to wind down.

So, what is the answer? Coaching. We need mentors, trainers, teachers and coaches in every aspect of our lives to keep us focused and active. I made an appointment with a counselor to discuss balancing home and work and off the cuff I said, "So, who's your therapist?" He laughed and then gave me a name. I looked at him quizzically and asked if he was serious. He told me never to trust a mentor, coach or even a therapist that doesn't need a tune-up occasionally or even often.

It was our exchange that prompted me to generate this course. The therapist was right. There comes no time in anyone's life when they have ALL the answers, that they have reached the pinnacle in our ever changing and dynamic environments. Our world is moving quickly, perhaps my grandfather had a lot of answers thirty years ago when he was telling me a thing or two but he sure doesn't know how to text.

The point is, our world is changing constantly, swirling about us at such a rate it's a wonder any of us can function let alone find a way to succeed. For this very reason, we must forever be trying to find those who can help us to realize our own best and to teach us that "best" is an evolving concept. I'm here to help you attain your goals by amping your negotiating skills.

Without cheerleaders, coaches, mentors, therapists and people for us to admire and try to emulate, we can't continue to grow and learn. We do not live or exist in a vacuum. Don't be so arrogant to think you know it all. There is always more to learn and people to learn it from.

CHAPTER 3

**Kinetic Thinking Closes the Gap
Between Setting Goals and Attaining Them**

When was the last time someone asked you what your goals are? What did you say? Do you know what your goals are? Have you taken the time lately to assess where you are personally and professionally? Do you find goal setting intimidating or overwhelming? I have some tips to take the stress out of goal recognition and fulfillment. And, you guessed it, most every path to realization of a goal or fulfilling a desire requires negotiation.

Most people would start with a list, but I find lists to be disorganized and stressful. I tend to use a quadrant system for most everything. This way I can break up my list into four digestible parts. On a piece of paper draw a vertical line and intersect it with a horizontal line so you have four sections.

"What are my goals?" In what area of my life? Good point. That's the first task. Use the quadrants to separate the areas of your life in which you have goals.

Personal Goals should be listed in the top left quadrant: "Work out more," "spend more time with the kids," and such. **Business Goals**, in the top right: "Secure promotion," "start own business," for example. In the bottom left quadrant, list goals for **Enrichment**, such as: "Read 'The Seven Habits of Highly Effective People,'" "take a course on negotiation," "learn to make chicken Marsala." Reserve the bottom right quadrant for **Recreational Goals**, like: "go to Easter Island" or "take kids on cruise to Alaska."

Not all of us get to approach a goal with the single-mindedness of say, a running back or a center in hockey. One good reason is because often our goals are not as clear. When setting a goal, it is critical that it be as specific as "put the ball in the basket." If you don't clearly articulate a goal, whether it's personal or professional- it's impossible to develop a pathway. Once your quadrant is done use the points below to fine-tune your objectives.

1) I'd like you to take a moment and put an "N" next to the items on your quadrant you think will need negotiation. You'll be surprised how many do. If you're married,

you're going to have to negotiate almost anything that requires the use of money. You might have to negotiate with the kids about going to Alaska instead of Disney. Even starting your own business is likely going to involve many negotiations. If you're going to take on a partner, there's a partnership agreement, if you have to lease space or purchase it there will be negotiations with land lords or property owners, you will have to negotiate with the vendors who will help you to finish out your space, install your electronics and then of course your spouse who isn't going to be excited about you quitting your "real job" to start your own company.

2) The good news here is that I'm going to show you how to negotiate with everyone and the lessons you learn will help you with each and every negotiation you enter.

3) Be precise. Don't make blanket statements like "Make more money." While that might be a goal, it lacks structure. You need to be specific. "Crack open a revenue stream marketing customer service consulting to boutique hotels."

4) Be realistic. While I want to be an NFL player, it simply isn't realistic at forty-two. Yes, I can train. Yes, I can try to walk on like Marky Mark in "Invincible," but is it likely to happen? Is this a good use of my time? If I won the

Heisman but decided to take some time off to become an attorney, get married and have a few kids and I now want to pursue my goal of playing in the NFL, it might be a good time in my life to give it a crack. I guarantee a negotiation with the wife. However, if I've never played football but LOVE watching it, this is likely an unrealistic goal. Be honest with yourself. It will save you time and emotional energy. Eliminate unrealistic goals.

5) Is your goal meaningful? I want to run a four-minute mile. Why? It's nearly impossible. Am I a runner? No. Do I like to run? Not particularly, at least not enough to actually achieve such a strenuous goal. The chances of me actually devoting the time necessary to set a world record are minimal. Scratch all goals off your quadrant that aren't deeply motivating or meaningful to you. I just found out my boss is pregnant, and she always told me she'd never return after having a child. That gives me nine months to become her replacement. Time for Kinetic thinking. There will be a negotiation looming.

6) You've decided (after intense negotiations with your wife) to become a real estate investor. Her issues were that none of your money be used to acquire properties as you've have been saving for the children's college. NO PROBLEM!!! I have a course that specifically outlines how to use private lenders to run your entire real estate portfolio. The best news here is the techniques covered in

this negotiation course will help you to meet the negotiated requirements of your wife by negotiating with private lenders. Everything in life is a negotiation.

The Kellams Theory of Kinetic Thinking is about finding a way. No matter what the goal, you must create a strategy. There is a great distance between setting a goal and attaining it and quite often it involves negotiating. Kinetic thinking is the first step to closing the gap. I'm going to say this many times during this course, because I want you to internalize it. The most prepared person generally prospers in a negotiation.

Just like a punt returner, you are looking down field toward the goal and formulating a way to get there. Some people see obstacles and some people see holes, pathways. When running the ball back for a touchdown, there is little opportunity to recognize or celebrate milestones, but you can be certain it's being done (fifty yard line, twenty, goal line). There are always these small victories during a negotiation. While you need to recognize them, do not get too cocky (until it's over and you have what you want. Try only to gloat in private).

To make sure your thoughts are always active and engaged, identify hallmarks for the path to your goal and make sure you not only recognize them when they have been achieved but take time to reflect and energize yourself for the rest of the run. Negotiations are about milestones and you will notice your attitude and mood change as you accomplish certain goals and if you should lose a point for now.

NOTES

CHAPTER 4

How to Create Authority
"The Kellams Theory of Kinetic Thinking"

We've seen it time and again throughout history, the inherent need to follow, to believe in someone, something.

Regardless of the field in which you desire to prosper, you must become an authority. So, this is a goal and once a goal is put into place there is no room for insecurity, incompetence or timidity. How do I get from "here" to "authority." A plan must be formulated and the kinetic thinking begins.

First, your goal must stay at the forefront of your mind by actively educating yourself in the field. This goes far beyond reading and research. This includes finding out who the leaders in the field are and getting close to them, friend them, become friends and learn everything you possibly can about the field.

Active thought requires you to DO. You must go to conferences, seminars, attend lectures given by those who dominate your field. The confidence you gain daily will translate into pure supremacy to those around you.

Once you become an authority, you are in a much better position to negotiate. Not that you would intentionally try to intimidate the other party, but I can guarantee Donald Trump doesn't do much negotiating. He is a mogul and he tends to get what he wants. Few people are on his level in the real estate business, but if you come to the table looking sharp, confident and prepared, you have an advantage.

Negotiations are games. Often there are winners and losers, but this is not necessarily so. Your goal should always be a win/win resolution. This is evidence you are fair and ethical and this is how we build relationships.

Let's say you are negotiating the purchase of a duplex from someone and you have a smooth and cordial sale. This shows good will and when he is ready to sell again or if you determine you might like to buy from him again, you have an established relationship and that can benefit you.

CHAPTER 5

How These "INs" Can Cause you to be Out Negotiated

What factors can generate barriers to a successful negotiation?

INsecurity is a huge hurdle in the pursuit of any goal at the negotiating table. Once you determine a clear and concise goal it's necessary to examine the elements your character that will help you on the path to success. Identifying your insecurities will help you to find a way around them.

If your goal is to successfully acquire a high net worth individual as a private money lender, you might start smaller so you can hone your craft with people who will be more likely to trust you with their money to invest. Practicing negotiating will lead to confidence. The more confidence you have, the less insecure you will feel.

INcompetence is a perfect roadblock to reaching a goal in a negotiation. Do NOT ever go into a negotiation without information. This is not the time to shoot from the hip, you will likely lose. In order to gain competence, begin using the tactics in this course to start negotiating your daily life. The more competent you become in your negotiating, the greater changes you will have of negotiating the bigger deals.

Once a goal is set, one enemy of negotiating is INdecision. Imagine a quarterback receiving the ball from a shot-gun formation and seeing several options roll out before him. Not being prepared and able to decide which path to take will result in failure. You need to prepare a strategy based on what your desired outcome is and how you intend to reach it. The way to eliminate indecision is preparedness and the way to become prepared is to embrace Kinetic thinking. Learn. Research. Do.

INdifference has no place in a negotiation. If you are indifferent to the objective- it will not be met. There must be a driving force toward meeting the goal. Frankly, no one wants to negotiate with someone who doesn't want to negotiate. If there is no room for movement- coming to the table is pointless.

For example, you want to buy a house you see as a perfect investment. You leave a little note for the owner letting them know you'd be interested in offering him a generous price. You don't hear from the owner. You try again. Finally, driving by you see one of the neighbors raking leaves and stop to chat. What does she know about the owners? You learn the man's wife recently passed, in the home and he hasn't been out much. Family has stopped to check on him but they don't see him EVER selling the house. In this case, chances are there is little reason to pursue it at this time. This doesn't mean you can't reach out again periodically, but knowing the man's wife passed in the house increases the chance he will not want to leave it. He is currently indifferent as his heart is not interested in selling.

Being completely INflexible is impossible as you begin negotiation. I am not saying there won't be points you are unwilling to concede- there will be. However, you must have your list of items you consider flexible and be willing to concede them. There will be stumbling blocks, the course of the negotiation might be changed for reasons beyond your control, set backs are almost a guarantee so being rigid and unwilling to compromise will spell defeat.

CHAPTER 6

Coming to the Table

In this game of life, we spend a great deal of time negotiating. It may seem as if negotiations only happen behind closed doors and often with the help of a mediator, but this is untrue.

When was the last time you asked your boss if you could leave early? If she refused, were you able to convince her to allow you to shave a few hours off your day? Whether you did or you didn't convince her, you were engaged in a negotiation.

There are three hard and fast principles of negotiation:
1. You do it all day everyday with your children, your friends, your peers, business associates, bosses and even

sales people. Now that you recognize that, embrace it and PRACTICE. Negotiating can not only be fun, but doing it well will serve you well.

2. You must have a clear-cut objective before you even begin a negotiation. Even if it is to get your landlord to discount a portion of a month's rent due to a poorly executed service call, you need to begin with a goal in mind.

3. The person who is most prepared generally achieves their goals.

We negotiate to resolve an issue or issues. All negotiations involve the achievement of goals and the crux of the issue is there is more than one party negotiating and generally the goals conflict, which is why you are negotiating to begin with.

Before we get too deep, I want to discuss the word "concession." This is a point you give over to move closer to a resolution. I want to give you a simple example so when I say concession five thousand times in the next hundred pages you have a clear picture.

Here is an example of negotiating in real life. I want you to be aware of it moving forward. Every, single, time you find yourself negotiating I want you to be aware, present and active. Remember that job you hated before you decided to get into the exciting world of real estate? OK, so you have tickets to a concert you don't really care about going to. Your boss says, "I need you to work on Friday night." You remind him you asked for that night off because you (inflate the situation here because you are a brilliant negotiator) finally got the hottest chick on earth to agree to go out with you and you spent a fortune on concert tickets.

None of this is true. Your buddy gave them to you for free because he didn't WANT to go and you invited your cousin. The fact remains, you don't want to work, you'd rather stay home and play video games than work OR go to the crappy concert.

"I'll give you the next two weekends off," he tries to sweeten the deal. What? Does he think you are stupid? If you aren't working, you aren't being paid. You can't afford two weekends off, but since you have worked three in a row, you are looking forward to a Friday night off.

"No. I really want to take this girls out." Made up girl, because obviously your cousin is not hot and even if she was ...

"Listen. I really need your help here. I've asked everyone."

Since you are a pretty good negotiator by nature and understand never giving something for nothing, you counter. "Time and a half and a guarantee I get New Year's Eve off."

"You know I can't do that."

"No, I know you can't run the shift on Friday without me."

"Let me call (insert "higher authority" here." He likely isn't calling anyone, he wants you to think he's all for it (your "buddy") but doesn't want you to feel too powerful. "All right, you got it. Don't be late," he adds for good measure to let you know he's still the boss.

OK, for sure he didn't want to give you time and a half. He wanted to offer you things he "thought" you wanted, and it backfired because you didn't. He wanted you to be a "team player," but you held your ground and waited to see how desperate he was to get the shift covered. This was a very clever negotiation and you were stingy with your concessions. You used two "decoys" (we will talk about these later) the first was the concert you REALLY wanted to go to and the second was the HOT girl. Well done.

Ideally, this is how negotiations need to go. As I said, not all negotiations take place in the business setting, but for the purposes of this course, we are going to examine those that do, however, during the time you are working through this information begin mastering your craft. Negotiate things you don't need to negotiate. If someone asks you for something,

"Hey, can you drop these in the mail when you leave for lunch?" Think of what they could do for you. "Sure, as long as you can answer my phone while I'm gone. I'm expecting a really important phone call and I'd rather they speak to a person than my voice mail." Even if you aren't expecting a phone call, this begins to awaken your skills as a negotiator at the same time stopping people from assuming you are the go to person for their personal errands.

This is a simple example, but in practicing the art of negotiating, you will be surprised how quickly you become good at it and how naturally you do so.

CHAPTER 7

WHAT ARE IMPORTANT ACTION ITEMS PRIOR TO THE NEGOTIATION?

According to the Kellams Theory of Kinetic Thinking, there is a great deal that needs to be accomplished prior to a formal negotiation. I'm a great advocate of getting a jump on the competition by investing time, energy and thought.

Before you enter an official or business negotiation, lists are critical.

- Make a list of what you will not compromise on, in other words, what you are setting out to achieve.
- Make a list of issues that are not important to you, the concert and your date, from the above scenario, but might be important to the other party (we will discuss that later).

- Next is a list of what you believe the other party wants to accomplish.
- A final list will have items on it you believe are unimportant to them but important to you. Why? This goes back to the Kellams Theory of Kinetic Thinking. The more prepared you are, the better chance you have of winning your negotiation.

1. In the interest of presenting yourself an authority, you need to have a very clear understanding of your business, your philosophy, your goals, your desires and your plans for the future of your business. Be prepared to discuss your accomplishments and your commitment to the community and or the environment. You never know how many other people are vying for the property you are negotiating for so giving the other party a good look into your business might help you to develop a rapport from the onset.

2. It's also important to know your limitations. How far are you willing to go and at what point are you going to either walk away or threaten to conclude the negotiation. We will talk more later about "walking away" and what a "dead-lock" means. In most every negotiation you will have restrictions. These could be financial restrictions, time restrictions, contingencies regarding other deals- whatever they may be, make sure you consider all of

them. It could be as simple as knowing exactly how much repairs are going to cost and not being able to move below a certain offering price. Knowing your restrictions and limitations will give you a solid base of knowledge regarding what you can and can not concede.

3. Not all negotiations, even over real estate, have money at the core. I'm reminded of the movie "Two Weeks Notice" in which Hugh Grant was playing a Donald Trump type character. He wanted to knock down a block of the neighborhood where Sandra Bullock lived. Within that block was the senior center where her father and his buddies played cards and got together to tell war stories. Ninety minutes later, at the end of the movie, Hugh and Sandra were in love and he had developed the property and preserved the senior center. Of course, that is fiction, but the point is, not every negotiation is about money and you need to be aware of such.

4. Research the other party. Knowing who is most invested can be a powerful tool.

5. Make sure you know all terms that may be negotiable. Interest rate, financing options, who will handle the title work, what the repair and rehab costs are going to be and not the least of which, how much you plan to make on the

deal once it is done. You need to know if you are willing to take less to get the deal done.

6. Research their businesses. Know everything about their company and philosophy. You should know your competitor as well as you know your own company. They will most definitely feel a bit intimidated by this and while we are not trying to intimidate, we ARE looking to position ourselves as authorities.

7. Find out if they have any judgments against them. This could be what is motivating the sale of a property.

8. Talk to people who know them, but do it in a harmless way. Inquire rather than interrogate.

9. Run a background check if you are able to do so.

10. If you know people who used to work with them, speak to them. If the seller used to work at Kinko's, he probably was rarely in a position to have to do any serious negotiating, but if he was a loan officer of a large an successful bank, you can count on having a negotiator at the table.

11. Google them and know everything about them. It's frightening how much you can find out on the internet.

12. If they have a blog (personal or business) read it. Personal blogs often give you insight into the way a person thinks, what they value and what drives them. You can often also get an emotional framework, which you could use in negotiations.

13. Find out everything you can about their family. This can expose Achilles heels (points of weakness). A great example here is knowing the person with whom you are about to negotiate has just had twins. You have an advantage because likely he is tired, not excited about an extended negotiation, he probably lies awake at night thinking about financing two weddings, private school and college. Of course they will both go to medical or law school because the twins are brilliant. He's likely looking to free up some cash.

14. Get to know the person or the company as far out from negotiation as possible, this could give you an edge. The closer you get to the actual negotiation, the closer people keep their cards to the vest. I actually once had a friend who closed a highly lucrative real estate deal because he had gone to The Juilliard School, which is the undisputed school for the arts. My friend had majored in music and a vocal chord injury shortened his career, but at the outset of negotiations, through some friendly discussion he learned

the other party's daughter was applying and getting into Juilliard was her life long ambition.

My friend agreed to come and watch a few performances and was truly impressed. He offered (was not asked) to write a letter to the Dean of the drama department. On that letter alone, the deal was sealed, a long-term relationship was formed and after his daughter was accepted, likely on her own merit, her father became my friend's most valuable high net worth private lender.

15. Know every aspect of the business you are negotiating. If you are negotiating terms with a private money lender for a property he is interested in investing in make sure your proposal is clear, concise and complete. He will be impressed with your knowledge and preparation and it will be easier to acquire him as a lender.

16. Try not to take the negotiation personally. Remember, both parties are at the table to act in their own self-interest.

17. If you are attempting to purchase a property, you need to know EVERYTHING about it. How long has it been on the market or has it been? When was it taken off the market? What is the asking price? Don't be afraid to inquire as to the balance of the loan- you'd be surprised what people will offer up in the way of information.

When was the roof last repaired or replaced? All these things will be points of negotiation later so DO YOUR HOMEWORK!

18. Know the deadlines you are working under and if possible, know the other party's deadlines as well. You will find, the bulk of resolution comes fairly close to the deadline. Know whether you can renegotiate your deadline if the goal you want to achieve is not achieved.

19. I like to request that all decision makers are involved in the negotiation. I'll explain why. A skilled negotiator will always have someone they have to "run things by" or a "committee" they need to present the offer to- in negotiation terms this is called a "higher authority." Sometimes they are real, and sometimes they are made up.

    Whether it's big business or small business, it is generally a tactic, so at least request it- you never know, Aunt Cecily might indeed end up at the table and make a blunder by hitting her nephew and tell him to take that first ridiculously low offer you throw out. After all, she is eighty and wants to live out her golden years on that $100,000 you just offered her for her plantation that's worth at least $250,000 after repairs (which will likely be significant). It never hurts to ask.

20. I like to request negotiations on Fridays. No one wants to be locked in a room all day when they are thinking about the weekend. Further, they are more likely to strike a deal at the ninth hour on a Friday instead of fretting about the deal over weekend.

21. If there are more people on your team (business partners or such) than you, make certain all team members are on the same page. You can't have any cracks in the armor. No one can speak for anyone else, over anyone else or make concessions that have not been previously discussed. If you need to confer with your team, you need to step outside or ask the mediator for some privacy.

> I have a horrible story to illustrate this point. A buddy of mine wanted to open a full-service day spa. There was a large and profile plaza in a posh area of Dallas. When he met with the leasing agent, the agent told him in "secret" that Ritz-Carlton had already drawn up plans to open a flag-ship hotel literally outside the front doors of a much larger space than he and his partner were considering.
>
> The leasing agent brought over plans and showed them, convinced them taking on four thousand square foot would be like printing

money. The hotel had no plans to put in a spa and there was no end to the retail they could offer in their luxurious space. The sales job was compelling so they signed a five-year lease.

The hotel was a year and a half out from the time of leasing so the leasing agent offered no rent increase for the term of their lease. All was right in the world until the ground never broke. Restaurant after restaurant opened instead and soon the plumbing of the plaza was OVERWHELMED by the preponderance of restaurants and clubs.

At least two days a week the spa had to be closed due to sewage and fumes coming up through the toilets and sinks. After it was clear no hotel was coming, the partners conferred and hired an attorney to break their lease and ask for their previous three years rent to be returned. There would be a request for lost revenue as well.

The attorney was ecstatic as he saw the payout increasing every day as he researched the deceptive business practices and located other merchants who were promised the same. There were ten plaintiffs named- some as big as MetLife and CHUBB and the attorney saw a huge payoff. He cautioned the partners a negotiation of this magnitude could last up to two years, but he'd ask for all of that money spent to be returned with damages.

The day of negotiations, the lead attorney for the plaintiffs opened with a letter he'd received not from my buddy but his partner siting poor economy and flagging business as a reason they were pleading to be let out of their contract. There was no mention of the hardship or revenue lost or even the potentially hazardous work conditions bubbling sewage created. He didn't mention lying or scheming on the side of the leasing company or the plaza owner, it was a clear cut begging and pleading to be released. He admitted vulnerability, poor business practices and appealed to sympathy. WRONG.

The negotiation ended there as the plaintiffs refused to pay any damages but did release them from their obligation, but they had to be out within ten days. Now, insult to injury they had no place to do business for the months it took to acquire new space and build it out. Needless to say, they are no longer partners or friends and this clearly illustrates why all parties must be in agreement and have full-disclosure of who has been told what and what documents have traded hands.

When you have a team negotiation is it critical you know all information that has been released and to whom. All of this must be made transparent prior to the negotiation table. Had my buddy's attorney known about that letter- he'd have taken a different tack that didn't include five thousand dollars in mediation fees.

CHAPTER 8

WHAT IS MOTIVATING THE NEGOTIATION?

Knowing what is motivating someone to buy or sell can be a valuable tool at the negotiation table. Is the property nearing foreclosure? Has the seller lost his job and can no longer afford the property and simply needs to get out from under it and is willing to forego some equity? Is there a divorce pending? Does the seller need the equity to render care to an ailing parent? Is bankruptcy looming? All these things give you power at the table. While I don't want to seem unscrupulous knowledge always has been and always will be POWER.

On the flip side of this, know what is motivating you as the buyer. If you could take or leave the property, you are in a position of power. If it is one of may properties you are looking at, but the seller is highly motivated you are in the driver's seat because you are willing to walk away if you don't get the terms or the price you are asking.

CHAPTER 9

THE RISKS INVOLVED IN ANY NEGOTIATION

When we talk about limitations and such, know your risks going in. There is always the risk a deal will not be struck, so know how that plays into your future plans. There is always a risk the deal you wanted will not be what you hoped for- this is not a reflection of your prowess as a negotiator, sometimes deals can not be done for unknown reasons. Perhaps we never did uncover what was motivating the other party. Perhaps he wanted part of the property reserved for a city park and that wasn't within your development plans.

Try not to see failure in a negotiation that doesn't yield the desired results. Why? Because I firmly believe there is good news in every bad news. I heard a story the other day about a man who was involved, vaguely in an SEC (Security and Exchange Commission) scandal. He served a short (slap on the wrist) sentence that saved him from being killed in his office in the first World Trade Tower that was hit. His actual office was on the floor where the plane entered and everyone from his firm was killed.

This is not new age thinking or even meta-physical blathering- when one door closes, another opens. When I ask you to have a clear idea of your limits and the concessions you are willing to make, I do it for a reason. It's too easy to get caught up in the "game" or the "desire to WIN."

When I go to Vegas, I like to gamble as much as the next person, however, I set limits for myself and I have a system that works for me so I can take in the strip and enjoy myself. It's a lot like negotiating. I take the amount of money I'm willing to lose and put it in my back pocket. I only take one hundred dollar bills because that helps to create a climate at the black jack table. I put one, one hundred dollar bill in my front right pocket where people keep their small change (right?).

I come up to the table and watch it for a while to make sure everyone is playing by the rules. Every game has rules and so does every negotiation. In negotiation you never GIVE without GETTING. In gambling, if you give and give and give and get nothing back, it will be the same as a failed negotiation- the bottom line is you LOSE.

So, if I see the people at the table playing by the rules, much as you want to see fair and ethical people at the negotiating table, I put my hundred dollar bill (my opening bid- strong and confident) on the table and receive my chips. My chips are MY bargaining pieces. I can give as much as I want and I can even give more if I see things going my way mid-stream. I

If you aren't familiar with black jack, there is a point when you are allowed to double your bet if you think you might beat the dealer and also a point when you can split your cards and match your bet to see if you can win both hands.

So, I play by the rules and I lose. Everyone else played by the rules. Some won, some lost. I put all the chips I win in my front pocket and play out what is in front of me. When my playing chips are gone, I leave the table. I resist the urge to pull from my winnings or continue no matter how "hot" the table might be. I then go to a new casino and do it all over again. In my experience I tend to end up 30% up. Why? FANTASTIC QUESTION!!!!

- I knew what I was willing to LOSE.
- I evaluated the playing field and didn't come to a table that was not following the rules.

- I preserved my winnings and didn't play with them, thereby knowing I'd walk away from the table a winner- as to how much I'd won I wouldn't know until I cashed in.
- I resisted the urge to take more money out of my pocket and keep playing no matter how high my spirits or moral were.
- I was able to walk away when the money I could see was gone.

How does that relate to a negotiation? Another fantastic question.

- You know going in, because you have prepared exhaustively, what you are willing to give up and what you are willing to concede.
- You approach the table confidently and prepared to meet your opposing parties.
- You have done your research on them, their properties and their company so you have a reasonable expectation of their "power" and what they are actually willing and able to concede or offer.
- You are friendly and winsome in nature automatically putting the other party at ease. No one wants to be at the table with a barracuda.
- You keep your cards close to the vest, not letting anyone know where you stand at any particular time and what your next move is.

- You negotiate only with what you planned for in the beginning, you don't suddenly start making calls to private lenders or parents or partners in order to secure a property because you want to WIN.
- You must divorce yourself from the concept of WINNING. It is not about winning, if it is, you need to be prepared to lose.
- You are willing to get up from the table if suddenly people stop playing by the rules, if you reach a point you see a dead-lock or you have determined nothing will be resolved on that day.
- WHEN IS LOSING ACTUALLY WINNING? Well, if you didn't get exactly what you wanted in a negotiation, it isn't a failure. Often times, you end up with a tax write off that was much needed, or your short-term "loss" that will turn into a long-term gain.
- Don't get so wrapped up in what YOU WANT that you can't negotiate at all. It's a give and take.

CHAPTER 10

THE FACE-TO-FACE NEGOTIATION

There are many reasons for face-to-face negotiations, the first of which is it's harder for people to say no to you in person than it is over the phone or via email.

Telephone calls can be interrupted several times resulting in loss of momentum, forgetting a crucial point or simply the desire to get off the phone. Additionally you don't have the benefit of reading body language, which can be critical in a negotiation. We will discuss body language more later.

Silence on the phone can easily be misinterpreted. You can't see the expression on the other person's face, thereby you don't know how they received your offer or statement so you can't regroup effectively. Silence is an effective strategy, it shows you are thinking person and you are thinking before speaking. Most people do not employ this in life let alone in business. There seems always to be a rush to communicate. Most people do not like dead air, there is an innate desire to fill the space with words.

There is the benefit of a firm handshake and eye contact that puts the other party at ease and makes them feel you are an honest and invested party. Picking up the phone shows a lack of effort, sincerity or interest.

If you must negotiate over the phone, make certain to write a clear agenda regarding what you want to accomplish. Try to stay on task and make sure you go back to your agenda each time you stray from the topic.

I recommend NOT trying to negotiate over lunch- the lunch hour is generally limited both for the restaurant and those dining. The waiters and wait staff tend to try to rush your meal to get another table during that hour and a half window. You will be interrupted repeatedly, momentum will be altered and you might over look important issues.

The golf course or dinner can be a good place to do business, but not necessarily to enter a tough negotiation.

Make sure you bring your above referenced lists so you don't forget anything and ALWAYS take notes whether you are on the phone or in person. This will prove critical if you have to resume negotiations at a later time or if there is an interruption. I like to have the notes recorded and send a copy to the other party.

CHAPTER 11

THE POWER OF READING
THE OPPOSING PARTY

People are by nature or nurture timid or bold. This can play a large role in a negotiation. Those who are timid try to avoid conflict and tend to be "people pleasers." Detecting this in your opponent is a gift if you are more bold. The timid are much more likely to make concessions to "get it over with" and often times can be seduced into re-evaluating on the fly.

The bold are almost always in the position of power because they are not afraid to be assertive, to make demands, to demean, however, this is not always the tack taken by one who is bold. If one is both bold and clever, he is likely an observer. He will size up the "competition" and make some assessments that will help him to make calculated moves in the game of negotiating.

- If the opposing party seems to lack confidence, the bold party will soften his approach and mirror the other party's posture and demeanor. This is a powerful method of putting people at ease. Flattery will come next but it will not be so blatant as to be off putting of obvious.
- Getting to know the other party can help to find the chink in the armor where you might be able to insert a blade. Begin a bit of conversation about your dad and how driven he was and the pressure he put you under. If the other party responds in kind, you can likely surmise he never feels good enough and is always trying to prove something. Telling him he drives a hard bargain or that his father "taught him well," will keep the moral up while you plot your final blow.
- If you begin soothing his bruised emotions, he will begin to like you and even if the outcome is not exactly what he'd hoped for, he likely will not come out of the negotiation feeling he's lost. The goal is win/win and coming out feeling like you held your own with a skilled negotiator who ultimately won, still feels pretty good to someone who feels like they have come up short most of their lives.
- Remind the opposing party they have choices and options, heck, with your two brilliant minds together all issues can

be resolved. Little does he know you came in with a long list of options and concessions and choices for him, but let him lead himself to water, after you make him thirsty.

BODY LANGUAGE AND HOW TO READ IT

Body language, called Kinesis (kin-E-sis), is very important in a negotiation and far too few people actually pay attention to that of their opponent. We tend to be so concerned with how WE are feeling and processing OUR emotions and working through the negotiation, we don't realize how much power is sitting in front of us. I will caution you not to send out any of these signals either.

- Rolling of the eyes can be a strategic move similar to what people call "flinching." It's a response to an absurd offer or a silly concession. It lets the other person know they are going to have to do better. In other cases, it can annoy, frustrate and irritate the other party. If that is your goal, then you are on the right path, but if keeping things diplomatic is your goal, this is not a good idea.
- Rubbing hands together can send two different signals: nervousness or arrogance. Have you ever seen someone clasp their hands together in victory and nearly foam at the mouth over the impending money? Just know what you are communicating and if this is a gesture you do out of nervousness, try to keep your hands off the table.

- Folded arms across the chest is traditionally a defensive posture- however, if the other party is rubbing their arms, they might simply be chilled so don't make assumptions.
- Try to maintain eye contact at all times. It can unnerve people who are not bold, or create good will with those who are committed to a cooperative settlement.
- Do not rest your chin on your hands, it indicates boredom and is very rude.
- Pulling at your collar can suggest anxiety or simply discomfort after a long day of negotiating.
- Try not to fidget and keep note of the other party. Are they fidgeting? If so, why? Are they nervous or is this a habit?
- Steepled fingers give the appearance of supreme confidence. If you feel supremely confident, that is fine, but keep in mind what it is communicating. Don't be too sophisticated when you want to be on the other party's level.
- Linking is an interesting concept that while isn't a direct "body" language indicator it does involve language. Try to avoid linking a positive statement to a negative one by using the words, "but," or "however." Try using "and." Once you teach your listener you are not going to link negative and positive statements, they will listen more clearly. Examples of this are:
  - "I really appreciate your throwing in the new AC unit, ... logically we assume a "but" will come there and perhaps

the rest of the statement will be, "but you are still going to have to do better on your offer."

- "I really appreciate your throwing in the new AC unit, and I'd like to move on to the issue regarding ..." Save the "but" for later- a new issue.

It simply sets a different tone. Also, be careful using pre-amble. This is any statement that is designed to set up another.

- If you say things like, "I may just be a boy from Cut-n-shoot, Texas ..." the listener still recognizes this as a statement that will set up something. They know you are going to say something that undermines the issue at hand. "I may just be a boy from Cut-n-shoot, Texas but I can see a bad deal as well as anyone."
- "Now, I know you aren't going to like this offer, but ..." Just skip the lead out. Or, rephrase with, "I want this property, so I'm hoping you will have some ideas as to how we can come closer together."

CHAPTER 12

WHAT IS NEURO-LINGUISTING PROGRAMMING?

Neuro-Linguistic programming was developed by a Gestalt Therapist and computer programmer named John Bandler and a linguist and therapist by the name of Dr. John Grinder. It's an approach to communication, personal development and psychotherapy. As the name suggests, this is an approach to incorporating neurological processes ("neuro"), language ("linguistic"), and behavior that have or can be learned and applied to aspects of life.

In devising this training method, the men studied three well-respected therapists and began to model what they felt was each person's method and why that method worked so well. One was a hypno-therapist, one was a Gestalt therapist and the other a family therapist.

A great deal of time went into the development of NLP and it has become a widely used model for utilizing powerful psychology concepts and incorporating them into almost any aspect of life. Businesses rely on NLP for buying, selling, intra-office relations, and business to business relationships as well as client relations management.

If you find you are negotiating with someone trained in NLP you will have a distinct disadvantage. I personally think NLP is a worthwhile investment of time and the practical applications are tremendous in the business community.

I must tell you, NLP is not widely accepted by the psychiatric or medical science communities. Each person who goes through the training takes different skills away from it, but as you know, I am a proponent of learning, experiencing and find NLP to be a fascinating addition to business training and development.

I could go so deeply into NLP and using body language as negotiation techniques but they are in my opinion, sciences unto themselves and at this basic negotiation level, this course will get you where you need to go.

CHAPTER 13

THE POWER OF THE
EMOTIONAL CLIMATE

I find it important to establish an emotional climate if possible. I like to begin with some light banter- I've already found out where my "other party" went to school or where he's from (you'd be surprised what you can find out on the internet) so I open with, "How do you think the Red Raiders are going to do this year?" or "Didn't someone tell me you were from Oklahoma? I was born there, still have a lot of family there."

Show an interest in the person. Let him know you are friendly and want this to be a negotiation that ends in mutual satisfaction. In any real estate negotiation, you are going to be arguing terms (and there are a lot of them) so there is plenty of room to offer concessions. You've already established what you are willing to concede and the concessions that don't matter to you but might matter greatly to him. You'd be surprised what is important to one person that isn't important to another.

Quickie negotiations are not the norm, so manage your own expectations and prepare for a marathon over a sprint. Make clear to yourself you have many points of contention but have prepared yourself to be victorious and now it is time to head into battle. Blustery and defensive is pointless. Rushing to settle is showing weakness.

Patience and thoughtfulness shows caring and interest in the other party's perspective. You never know, they might actually come up with something you hadn't thought of and it could change the direction of the negotiation in a positive way. Make sure to acknowledge his contribution and approach the new avenue with enthusiasm. The goal, again is win/win when ever possible.

While every negotiation is a competition in a sense, it need not be combative or negative. I find the most successful resolutions happen when the emotion is removed from the negotiation. Business is business and you can't be insulted someone wants your property for less than you want to sell it for. After all, it is an inanimate object. Think about street markets where all things and all prices are negotiable- you don't see anyone getting angry you only want to pay fifteen dollars for their "hand-woven" quilt. This is where you often see a take-it-or-leave-it stance (we will discuss this later).

Further, keeping calm shows you are not highly motivated, this could lead to the other party making concessions early and this is how you get a sense (if you don't already know) of how motivated they are.

Some people negotiate for sport, but I caution you against being greedy- many sales are lost over wishing you had done better or trying to. What do I mean?

My neighbor told me he'd inherited a home in a small town near where I lived and had long wanted a lake house. He bragged it was paid for and what it was valued at after some repair and maintenance. I knew he was hoping to expand his business and cash would help him out a great deal. I offered him a price that was more than fair and he countered with an absurdly high number. It was several thousand over the fair market value. We haggled, I came a bit closer, he came down.

Neither of us were particularly motivated so they negotiations dragged out a few weeks during which time, another home on the same lake came available. The seller was highly motivated and was willing to take well below market value so he could put money down on a new build. I offered him far less than I offered my friend and he accepted.

When my buddy decided to come down a bit he was shocked and offended I'd gone another direction. Deal with people who WANT to negotiate. He was greedy and frankly was taking advantage of me because he knew I had the money. The real estate market imploded weeks later and he is still sitting on the lake house and has not had the capital to expand his business. Isn't greed one of the seven deadly sins?

Negotiations can and should be cooperative if possible. Don't get me wrong, I've been in some HEATED negotiations and mediations. Money is an issue that generates strong emotions. However, it is often the case what you THINK they other party wants is not what they actually want. We tend to see what we WANT as what they WANT. This doesn't mean you spearhead your objective by making the first offer. There is an old saying, so old I have no idea who said it first, probably my grandpaw, "the person who opens negotiations usually loses."

This is absolutely not the case, however, I recommend opening, if you elect to, with a concession you think matters to them. This way, their spirits are lifted and they feel powerful. They are more likely to view you as interested in a win/win negotiation. Their level of expectation increases markedly and they tend to come back with something that might be critical to you, but they don't know that. Let me illustrate what I mean.

> David James comes into a real estate negotiation with me. He knows the foundation of his home is a nightmare and is fearful it will be a sticking point. I already know the foundation is jacked and so is the house for that matter, but I plan to knock it down and build a duplex.
>
> My brother is a contractor, he's going to do the work for free and live in one half of the duplex with his fiancée. David knows none of this. So, I am going to let him start the negotiations by offering a price and then I am going to let him know I am aware that the ARV (after repair value) of the house is WELLLLLL below the asking price. I will delineate the problems with the property, the estimates I have gotten from contractors to make it livable.
>
> I'll tell him I know the house is paid off and offer him an obscenely low cash price with no constraints. He was testing the waters giving himself room to negotiate, but when he saw cash in the hand and no delays with financing- he snapped it up. Though he didn't get the price he wanted, he walked out with a check and was happy as a lark.

If you are the buyer and you offer the absurdly low price and they accept it without a moment of deliberation, you can pretty much be sure he is selling you a lemon and further research should likely be done before you jump in. This is where knowing all you can is critical.

In the real estate industry and in the current climate, it has been necessary for us to become masters of creative financing. For that reason, I see greater opportunity in negotiations because the game has changed.

People who have received bad loans and now find themselves in over their heads might be very open to a subject to loan where they literally deed the property to you and you make the payments. The title stays in the homeowner's name, which might cause problems for them in acquiring another home, but getting out from under their current mortgage and into perhaps something for lease might be very motivating. This preserves their credit and frees up the money that had been going straight to the house.

I'm seeing lots of equity rich properties selling for well under market value due to the fact the family's financial picture has been dramatically affected by the crashed economy. In this situation, it's easy to hold a cooperative negotiation by starting out sympathetic and understanding. These are highly motivated sellers and good reason for you to be a highly motivated buyer.

CHAPTER 14

THE POWER OF POWER

Sounds odd, right? Well, It's important to know, what you feel your power points are in the negotiation. It could simply be "I have something he wants." Just as important, you need to examine how he sees your power. Does he see weakness and if so, is there any weakness? Do you need to unload the property to pay a tax lien? Is the court forcing you to see all your assets to pay your spouse in a pending divorce?

No matter what, use your poker face and do NOT share any of this information. In the attempt to create a friendly climate- be very careful what you share. Nothing should give him any indication you are not in the position of power.

Another thing you need to acknowledge and perhaps focus on are the limits of the other party's power. They have limits- everyone does. Maybe he can not spend over a certain amount- this could give you an offer to ask for other concessions.

CHAPTER 15

THE POWER OF CHARISMA

If you are naturally charismatic (as actors and musicians tend to be) use your powers for the good of your cause. People tend to fall under the spell of those who seem to be who they wish they were. If you are attractive, use it. If you are funny, use it. If you are successful, never brag, but let them know you appreciate them coming to the table, you think "they," "their property," "their business" would be a fantastic addition to your "portfolio," "business," or even a place for your aging mother to live.

The warning I will give you about charisma is that it is not the same as confidence or arrogance, so if you are either of those things, don't assume you are charismatic. People like and want to emulate charismatic people, they tend to be repelled by arrogance and people who demonstrate offensive confidence.

If silence seems unnerving to the other party, turn on the charm- as long as you know how. Charisma is a strong personality trait. I know which of my students are going to be "natural born killers" in a negotiation because the other party wants to give in, wants to be friends, wants to be like them. It's a gift. I have other students who are charming and engaging and I see it help them at every turn, but charm is a different animal than charisma. The Pied Piper was charismatic- magnetic and hypnotic.

CHAPTER 16

THE DISADVANTAGE OF ASSUMPTIONS

You've heard the phrase, "When you assume you make an ass out of u and me." This is true. You can miss out on great opportunities at the negotiation table if you make assumptions about:

1. The property
2. The owner
3. The equity
4. The reason for selling
5. The goals of the other party

Making assumptions about any of the above could cause you to under or over bid. Both of which are not great openings. As

I've stated above, the way to eliminate assumption is to research. The information you are looking for is likely out there. If not all of it. Some of it. The more you know the better chance you have of being victorious.

Let's go back to our lists:

1. What you THINK they want
2. What you KNOW you want
3. What you would be willing to concede that will not affect your outcome
4. What you would be willing to concede that WILL affect your outcome
5. What you want that you don't think is critical to them

Why? This helps us to overcome our urge to assume. We are speculating but also being very clear about what we will and will not compromise on. Make sure you add in plenty of meaningless concessions (a refrigerator- you already have one), (lawn furniture- you hate it), (new carpet- your dad owns a carpet store and you can get it at cost though it would cost them 10k). The point to this is know exactly what you can offer and how gracious and cooperative it makes you look.

It's important, however, to be stingy with concessions that do cost you or that you do need to use to win more valuable points. I never begin a negotiation with the main issue I want to resolve.

This falls under negotiating 101- this tells the other party everything you will offer will be in order to obtain that item. In comes the "RED HERRING."

CHAPTER 17

THE TACTICS

Just the word "tactic" can have a negative connotation, mostly because it involves careful planning. Once you learn these tactics, you can use them to increase the probability of success in your negotiation. If you are entering a negotiation with a skilled negotiator, after this course, at minimum, you will be able to identify his tactics, the ones he likely uses on everyone and not fall for them and even use them against him.

CHAPTER 18

THE SILENT STRATEGY

Combining eye contact with a thoughtful gaze and respectful silence is powerful indeed. It gives your "opponent" the illusion you are evaluating what he is saying for it's worth to the negotiation. Little does he know, you are generally formulating your response as you'd already prepared for the speech in which he defends his position.

The less you say, the more he will say because people are uncomfortable with silence and want to fill it with any words. If he offers you a window into his personal life- jump on it. Mirror him, try to find out WHAT is motivating the deal you are negotiating. This might be the last piece of the puzzle.

By mirror, I mean, adjust your posture to be similar to his, talk about what he wants to talk about. I know, you might be thinking "time is money," but you'd be surprised how much can be accomplished when you slow down and invest some time in what the other person feels is important.

Always empathize and sympathize when you can. Share stories, make things up, do what ever you need to do to put him at ease. If he seems discomfited by your silence, say, "You know, you just reminded me of a deal I did ..." or "You got me thinking about something ..." This gives them the feeling you are genuinely interested. People feel valued when they are "heard" and listened to. Maintain eye contact and whenever possible use the other person's name. It makes them feel valued and important. They feel you are invested in this deal more than you are interested in "winning.

CHAPTER 19

THE RED HERRING OR DECOY

I recommend a list of items you could care less about and present them as critical. Such as the scenario stated above with the cracked foundation. Go on and on and on about what it would take to fix it and that alone makes the house virtually worthless. He doesn't know you are going to knock it down. He doesn't know what your real goal is- to acquire the property next to his own. Beat him down on the foundation and the general disrepair and show him your quotes and tell him it would cost more to make it viable than he is selling it for.

CHAPTER 20

THE OLDEST TRICK IN THE BOOK

You've seen it on every crime show since the dawn of time. The perpetrator has been brought in for questioning. The hot head cop starts brow beating the guy immediately trying to intimidate him, denying him comfort, using threats to try and get answers. Then he decides he's had it, wants to "throw the book at him," he storms out to get the Chief so they can start the process of "booking him."

The other cop pulls out a pack of cigarettes and offers the guy one. He calls out for a soda and asks the perpetrator if he wants something to drink. Then comes the apology for his partner's attitude, he gets really worked up. Then, he leans on the table, putting the guy at ease and says, "I want to help you, you don't have to take the fall for the whole …." So it goes on until the guy starts doling out information that implicates him.

People do this in negotiation all the time. It's easy to see and the best defense is to call them out on it. One partner will get up and throw his legal pad on the table and says, "I'm not dealing with this guy any more." The door slams behind him. This is when his partner smiles and apologizes. "Let's see what we can do to get this done. I see your points, all of them and I agree with you. I just know he won't budge on this one point. What are your thoughts?"

As I mentioned keep a third party in *your* back pocket. Though you've asked *them* to bring all the decision makers to the table, it might do you well to have someone you have to consult. If you don't feel you can force them to move off a point, step out of the room to regroup, fake a phone call, or if you feel you must, walk away.

It's important to know who is the most invested in the deal. If you feel you are, but don't perceive the deal getting done, don't be afraid to blame it on a "higher power" or your "inflexible, bad-cop partner." In some cases, this might be just what you need to force action. If the deal isn't critical, keep in mind there are many more deals out there. However, if you feel the other party is doing good cop bad cop, feel free to suggest terminating negotiations. This is often a great way to expose their tactic.

CHAPTER 21

BECAUSE THAT'S THE RULE

Don't ever be afraid to ask why. People love to create manuals and signs and price lists and such. This cuts down on having to answer the same questions over and over and over- but it also creates an air of legitimacy and inflexibility.

In a negotiation you might say, "I want the refrigerator for nine hundred instead of a thousand." Expect a no and a finger pointed to the PRINTED cost. Point out the small scratch on the side you know will butt right up against the wall in your new rental property and explain it's significant and they simply can't expect you to pay full price. You will likely get what you ask for.

I had a friend the other day who went to a large retailer to buy new washers and dryers for his new duplexes he's successfully negotiated a great deal on. He was flying high as he should have been and decided to work over the staff in the appliance department.

"Since I'm buying ten sets, I'd like a volume discount." Of course the sales person chuckled and said they don't offer volume discounts. He asked to see the manager who was out to lunch and no he couldn't be reached. So, he started to walk out. At that point, the sales man remembered his commission on the deal and told my friend he'd been able to reach the manager if he could just wait a second.

Ten percent was extended to him, which was great but he wasn't ready to stop. Every single item on the purchase agreement was challenged and each time he was told, "It says right here …" He threatened to take his business elsewhere. Each time he won.

I wouldn't say that if he'd only purchased one set he would have been able to negotiate such deals, but the point is, all terms are negotiable. Don't assume just because it's in writing that it is a LAW. Don't take a contract at its written words- challenge every point and see what you can get away with. Most people will not do this for many reasons.

- They don't want to inconvenience anyone
- They don't want to appear cheap

- They don't want to seem difficult to work with
- They don't want people to dread doing business with them because it always leads to a negotiation
- We have the "if you have to ask, you can't afford it" mentality and no one wants to appear as if they can't afford something.

Why do people write things down? Well, so they have something to refer to when you ask if you can … "Nope. It's on page six of the purchasing agreement. No free deliveries." Now, that doesn't mean you can't request it. It doesn't mean it is written in blood, or on a stone tablet- they might be able to concede it- given how much you have spent, how many people you have referred to them, how many times you have been a repeat client. Just because it's written, doesn't mean it can't be done.

It's a way for people to avoid negotiations. "It says right there on the wall, no …" The written word encourages us not to try to alter their way of doing business. Do you think the signs that people put in the windows of their homes and business that say, "No soliciting" stop people? No.

It is also a way to prove to people everyone is getting the same deal or paying the same price for things. Once again, it cuts down on negotiation.

In business and in life, time is money. Posting signs, writing manuals, having contracts and written rules cuts down on having to "consult the higher authority." By higher authority I mean the manager, the boss, the sales manager, the business owner or the bank president for that matter.

CHAPTER 22

TIME

Can be a critical tactic to use. When you begin, let the other person know, this deal is on the table today. I need to get it done or move on. This manages the expectations of the other party that they need to likely begin with the most important issues they have, which puts them at a bit of a disadvantage. You know what they want, what they need upfront- you know their vulnerable position and with that you can start giving in slowly on smaller concessions. This will boost their moral and make them believe this is going to be a cooperative negotiation.

Time is the most valuable commodity you have next to information when preparing for a negotiation. When you are given the time to do the necessary research, to compile reports and most importantly, to develop a strategy.

If you can construct a line of thinking for your opponent, you can, in advance prepare answers and counters for his objections. Put yourself in his shoes, think about what you would be thinking, how you would want the process to play out, the obvious questions and concerns and his sticking point. Now, do the necessary research to find two or three different answers, solutions and methods to resolve the sticking points. This is a very powerful tool.

Even if you are making a presentation to a potential investor or a potential private lender, you are still negotiating because they have not committed to you. The more thorough your proposal or presentation the better. If you can anticipate their concerns, fears, what they consider risks on the investment, what you can bring to the table, why you are the best person to invest with- the less time they will need to spend asking questions and challenging. This also goes back to establishing yourself as an authority.

If you come in with the air of authority, they will be more likely to give you their money, or sell you their property or purchase yours. As I said, I like to call a negotiation for a Friday, maybe an important Friday- if I know he has kids I try to pick the kids last day of school because often times it's time to get ready to go on summer vacation. Or, the Friday before a holiday weekend, or close to Christmas. I want them to come in with a "let's get this over with" attitude.

CHAPTER 23

KNOWLEDGE

Would you even consider walking into a job interview without knowing what you were interviewing for? That is as silly as coming to a negotiation without as much knowledge as possible.

You need to know the process. What is going to happen that day? Who will be attending? Will there be a mediator involved? It is critical to know every single aspect of the transaction that might take place. If you are going to buy a home, you need to know HOW you plan to do so. Have every bit of paper work at your fingertips. All appraisals and documents need to be present and orderly.

Have all your vendor estimations and quotes with you, if you have had the time to get a couple different quotes for the more expensive projects, bring them. If you are an established real estate investor, chances are you have vendors you have worked with time and again. You trust them, you believe in their product and work ethic. They are professional and timely.

Don't be afraid to defend that position if it comes down to what you are claiming is reasonable for repairs. Make sure the other party understands how much time has gone into getting these quotes, lining up a production schedule and securing valued customer discounts. Yes, there are cheaper companies, but you've been burned before by jobs that don't start on time, leaving other contractors unable to begin their portion, you have had contractors steal your deposits and never complete the jobs, you've had major errors on critical jobs that have caused extensive often irreparable damage.

Make sure you have prepared creative financing options incase traditional bank or mortgage company financing is not available. For more on creative financing through private lenders, see my course "Your Golden Tickets."

While you might not have any knowledge of the other party's limitations, you must assume there are some. Try not to spend all your time focusing on your own. Often fear of our limitations can stifle us a bit at the table. We don't want it to cause insecurity or to appear intimidated, so focus on what their limitations might be. The good news is likely they will be completely different so in most negotiations an agreement can be met. You are at the table for a reason- there is a goal, it's simply a matter of how you are both going to reach it.

CHAPTER 24

OPTIONS

Be prepared with options. If you are a real estate investor who does the bulk of your business with private lender money, make sure you have several investors tentatively committed to the deal you are negotiating. This will give you greater latitude. If the seller won't go as low on the prices as you thought, you likely will chose one private lender over another.

This is where it's critical to have an entire file on every one of your private lenders, so you never bring them a deal they wouldn't be interested in. Furthermore, I have a file on every person, in every field I do business with. You never know when you can put two people together, where they can profit hugely and you get the credit for the introduction.

Never under value the power of networking. I was in a negotiation once and the other gentleman and I got to talking about another deal he was working on and as it turned out, I am very close friends with someone he'd been trying to get in front of for five years. On break, I made a phone call to my friend (because everyone I do business with is a phone call away) and set up a lunch between them for the next day. I don't have to tell you our negotiation was over in three hours and we both left very happy.

CHAPTER 25

COMPETITION

How can you create competition? Every time you negotiate with a vendor or a contractor, be prepared with other quotes. I like to use down time do get general costs and specs on jobs I tend to repeat. Tiling, resurfacing of pools, foundation work, painting, grout- the basic repairs that help us to negotiate the price of a property whether we are buying or selling.

This makes people work harder to gain our business, it creates a desire on their part to be timely, efficient, honest, fair and the best. This way, they can insure further business. Never tell a contractor you are under a time bind and when can they get started? That gives the contractor too much power. Even if you are in a rush for quotes, get a few.

What if you have a hot deal on a property and you want to use a certain private money lender because he stays out of the deal, he doesn't want to see a proposal, he never asks questions- HOWEVER- he wants a percentage that is on the high end of the spectrum and it takes money right out of your pocket. Call him up and tell him about the deal but then say, "Oh man, I just got their offer and there is no way I can make this work if I'm giving you 15%. Sorry, I thought they were going to come in lower. Next time, buddy." He might jump at it. His money isn't working right now and it's better to make some than none.

CHAPTER 26

HOW DO YOU CUT DOWN ON YOUR OWN COMPETITION AND REDUCE NEGOTIATIONS?

Great question! There are several factors that can cut down on the competition you might have among private lenders and save you the time involved in negotiating.

- Your track record producing great returns on their investments will put you in front of other people vying for their money.
- The terms you offer should be fair and equitable.
- Build a relationship with your lenders. Get to know them. Create a comprehensive file that will allow you to touch base with them several times a year on birthdays and anniversaries so they like letting you use their money over

the next guy. Don't hesitate to shoot them an email when their alma mater is going well or even not so well and offer a gentle ribbing.

- The more professional you are, the better prepared you are for your first few deals the less negotiating you will find yourself doing with your private lenders.
- If you don't try to take deals to them that are outside of the terms they prefer, you won't have to negotiation much.

CHAPTER 27

THE RUN AROUND

When there is momentum going your way and the other party sees your mood elevating, he might try to use some random story or discussion to derail the issues at hand. In order to counter this, keep going right back to the topic at hand. If you must ask what the point of the story is, do so.

If you are a sports fan, imagine the quarter, half or period, heck, even the end of the game rapidly approaching and the other team is on FIRE. What does the opposition do? They draw a foul, feign an injury, call a time out, challenge a call, whatever it takes to interrupt the momentum.

It is a POWERFUL strategy, so make certain you don't stand for it. "I fail to see the relevance" is a polite way of ending the discourse.

CHAPTER 28

THE HOSTILE NEGOTIATOR

Often times, when the stakes are high, a company will send in someone who they think will hammer you until the deal is done. Don't be afraid to refuse to negotiate with that person and reschedule the negotiation until a replacement has been located.

Make it clear you feel uncomfortable with the climate and would prefer to reconvene when they can find someone who isn't so aggressive and intractable. Remember, it's a negotiation and there needs to be flexibility on both sides for it to be a negotiation and not a dictation.

CHAPTER 29

THE WALK OUT

It is not uncommon for the other party or even you to walk out. If it's you, re-evaluate the value of the deal and wait a month before you try to re-negotiate. This will give them time to do the same and clearly illustrate your willingness to lose the deal all together. Keep in mind, they are trying to demonstrate the same to you so they will wait a while as well.

THREATENING TO WALK OUT

Do not fall for this. If they threaten to leave the table, let them. Do not call them, do not try to resurrect the deal. If you don't respond to their "threat" they likely won't leave. Use your "silence tactic" to wait them out. You could even offer them a break to compose themselves.

Try not to pass the point where you can work out. If you get to where you are giving away too much and not happy with how things are looking, take some time to think things through.

If this leads to what is basically a "dead-lock" with neither party willing to budge, let some time pass. A dead-lock doesn't mean a dead deal. Often it takes the parties a while to process what happened in the negotiation and perhaps even to re-evaluate.

Wait some time and one of you will likely reach out. A difficult negotiation might require bringing in a skilled mediator or an unbiased third party to help.

CHAPTER 30

CASH IN HAND

So, the other party shows up (or you) with a cashier's check that is lower than the price you are negotiating AND a signed contract. This is a powerful tactic. "This is all the bank would give me. I love your house and I want it and I did the best I could." You have a choice right now.

Cash is King and cash in hand is very persuasive. The red tape has been cut through and you can either walk away with money or get a better deal on the property you were hoping for. You can still negotiate it if you want to risk losing the cash in hand just know whether it's worth it.

This is also called a "Fait Accompli." The person blames a higher authority or a timing issue on the fact he is coming to the table to buy that property he LOVES and wants so badly. "I know I'm three thousand short, but this is all the bank would lend me. We can wait for my mom to get back from Italy in a month to get the other three, but I'd really like to move forward. Can you work with me on it?"

Obviously there are a variety of options here. You can take away something you had conceded to earlier. "Sure, I will take that price but I can't replace the carpet." Or, you can cut and run to the bank with your money.

You could take that money and tell him he can finance the other three thousand, interest free over six months. There really is no end to what you can do here. What you simply MUST do, however, in this case is test the limitation they have tossed in your lap. Check the validity.

"Well, that's no problem. I have a private lender I can call right now and he can do a bridge loan for us. You can either pay him the note or we can call your mom and have her agree to pay the money upon her return from Italy." It's critical you verify the truth to their "limitation."

CHAPTER 31

JUST TRY IT FOR THE WEEKEND

I've done it and it worked beautifully. I had a couple coming into town to view a condo I was selling and he asked what area of town he should book a hotel so they would be close to great restaurants and not too far from the property.

I told him to stay at the condo itself. On me. Keeping in mind, this was a man who was well known among associates of mine, I knew the chances of him purchasing were fifty/fifty on a walk-through. The point is, I could trust him to stay in the property.

It was already furnished as I used it myself occasionally, so I simply inquired gently as to what type of things he and his wife enjoyed drinking. I made a quick stop at the store and loaded up the fridge with bottled water, wine, and easy to grab and go snacks.

This is similar to a car dealer letting you take the car for the weekend. He escalates your chances of falling in love with it. And yes, I sold the condo, furnished for what I was asking.

CHAPTER 32

WHY THE HELL NOT?

While it makes the most sense to try to come in close to an offer that might be accepted, why not try something totally different. Go in with an absolutely absurd offer NO ONE in their right mind would accept.

However, in doing so, you are automatically risking upsetting the other party, but what you are effectively doing is creating a situation where every other subsequent offer ends up looking better and better.

I like making that absurd offer and then tabling it for quite a while and going backward. Trying to elevate the "mood" and the cooperative spirit so when I go back to the offer and it is more reasonable and so much else has been worked out effortlessly, we are dealing with a totally different emotional framework in the other party.

Some people call this the "Bogey," I call it "why the hell not?"

CHAPTER 33

WHAT PISSES THE OTHER PARTY OFF IN A NEGOTIATION

This is an easy one. What would piss you off?

- Arrogance
- Condescension
- Assumptions
- Take-it-or-leave it right out of the gate. What is take-it-or-leave it? Exactly what it says. When one party leaves little room for negotiation by saying, "This is the price. Take-it-or-leave-it." There is GREAT power in leaving it and walking away from the table. No one wants their hand forced like that.
- Trying to renegotiate a previously offered concession. This is not going to be met with much happiness. Let me give you an example. Perhaps you are dealing with Aunt Susie's house and her nephew, Mark is handling the

negotiation. Already, he's told you he has FULL AUTHORITY. That means he is the DECISION MAKER. So, you throw numbers around, offer some concessions. He agrees to a price, maybe you break for lunch and then come back to hammer out the details during which time he tells you how embarrassing this is but Aunt Susie called during lunch to find out how things were going and was furious with the deal he had struck so it's back to the drawing board.

- Rudeness
- The basic principle is to keep things cooperative if possible.
- Avoiding eye contact
- Checking your watch or the clock
- Looking at your phone and or checking and responding to texts
- Ultimatums- are automatically inflammatory, do your best NOT to fall into this.
- Avoid using statistics. What do they say, "33.3% of statistics are inaccurate?" The point is, they don't do much but bog down your personal negotiation.
- Try not to break money down to absurd sizes. Such as, "Well, that is just two dollars a day!" It's annoying and frustrating.

Let's talk about AUTHORITY for a moment. This is a really interesting concept. As I mentioned earlier, I ask that all decision makers come to the table so we can hammer out a deal without a lot of external negotiating. However, it is a strategy to make sure that doesn't happen.

If you say you have FULL authority it means you needn't check with anyone- I don't recommend this because often times in a face-to-face negotiation it is essential to have to "run it by your boss," "partner," or the "board of directors." This maintains face and good will if you have to decline an offer. FULL authority is tough to manage.

If you stipulate, which I recommend, that there is a "decision maker" or a higher authority, someone you must run things past, you will never be stuck having to make a snap decision regarding an offer.

If you get the feeling the "higher authority" is running the show and not much is getting done, as if the "negotiator" is just a mouth-piece and more time is spend running to the phone, don't be afraid to push off negotiations until you can negotiate with the person in charge.

CHAPTER 34

The Never Ending Negotiation

Have you ever thought you were done and all the terms were decided and then the other party tries to start "nibbling?" In negotiating terms this is the person that says, well, if you are willing to throw that in, why not add ... The price has been accepted and suddenly the person says, "Well, I never buy a car without a full tank of gas," or "If I'm going to pay $5,000 for a wedding dress, I am going to need my veil and shoes thrown in."

You'd be surprised how often this works and often to your disadvantage. Once the tough negotiating has gotten done and you are ready to wrap up the deal, the last thing anyone wants is to go back and try and re-negotiate ANYTHING. It is not uncommon for the other person to "throw in" whatever it is the other party wants. It's not usually something huge or impossible, but they might come back around to that carpet they were unable to get you to budge on, or the new paint.

However, it's also a tool you might use yourself. It is generally viewed as unethical and the person doing it tends to look cheap and subversive. Additionally, people don't like to do business with someone after they have been "nibbled" to death. It's like going to dinner with that friend that nit-picks the waiter to pieces and sends his food back and ultimately asks for it for free. That dude is the "nibbler" and he'll do it in every negotiation. Exhausting.

Here is another example. You've agreed on the price of your car and you get to the table and suddenly you are hit with fifteen different add-ons, the sales person tries to "convince" you are absolutely critical. It is annoying and frustrating. This is "nibbling."

CHAPTER 35

THE HIGHER AUTHORITY

Is used in most every negotiation because no one wants to be "pinned down," or be the "bad guy." Further, if the other party thinks you have full authority, they will use every tactic out there to get you to move on issues. If you do not feel like you can hold your ground, bring a theoretical "higher authority" to the table.

While you have requested they bring all involved parties to the table so the deal can get done, you can always step out and make a call. If the other party does so, try to get him to commit on his own.

"If your boss is OK, with the terms at hand, is there any reason you wouldn't sanction a go ahead on this deal?" This way, if there really is a "higher authority" it gives you an idea of where you stand at that point in the negotiation. If he tells you he sees it as a go, other than this issue, stroke his ego.

"Well, I'm sure they always follow your recommendations, that's why they sent you here." Bolstering the other party's abilities is a great way to keep negotiations friendly and cooperative.

CHAPTER 36

GET OUT THERE AND START NEGOTIATING YOUR LIFE

I designed this course to let people know they DO know how to negotiate and that they do so every day. The more you practice, the better you become and the more confident you will feel.

I used to think only used-car salesmen and people who liked to "haggle" negotiated, but that is patently untrue. I want you to start small, but try it with everyone. Your wife, your secretary, your boss, your girlfriend, your children.

The focus of the concept is, "don't give anything away." I always get something when I give something and so can you. This course will get you started on your way to having more, gaining more, earning more and being more.

Made in the USA
Lexington, KY
17 May 2016